T0380855

Trunks, Snout, Nosey...
and the
Bright Shiny Stone

RW Rhodes
ILLUSTRATED BY TY HOOKER

Dedication

This book is dedicated to my three children: David, Amanda and Bobby. They are very different yet alike in many ways, and they are talented, special and dear to my heart.

I also want to thank my wife, Jolan who is the love of my life. She encourages me... to be me...and to live life to the fullest, and I do ... with her always at the edge of my thoughts.

In West Africa, along the Congo River, lived a
family of elephants....

Trunks

Snout

Nosey

Mom and Dad

They loved playing in the water in the Congo
River, splashing, squirting, swimming
and bathing.

Oh what great fun they had. Trunks, Snout and Nosey were the best of friends. And got along so well.

One day while playing in the river they spotted
a shiny round stone.

It was a bright shiny stone and they all wanted
it for themselves.

Trunks, Snout and Nosey were determined
to get the stone for themselves. They dived
into the river at the same time looking for the
bright shiny stone.

It's Mine said Trunks

"Let it go! It belongs to me. I saw it first," said
Snout.

"No way! it's mine. I saw it first," said Nosey.

Somehow the bright shiny stone was tossed
into the air.

Trunks grabbed for the stone but it slipped
away.

Snout leaped, grabbed it ,but tumbled into
the river. A huge wave came along and washed
away the bright shiny stone as it fell.

Nosey could not believe the stone was lost
again. She sat resting her head in the palm of
her hands crying.

The elephants were all sad because no one had
the bright shiny stone they were all
fighting over.

The elephants sat with sad faces staring
at the water.

Suddenly a Shiny twinkle of light appeared

Snout and Nosey swam toward the light and discovered that it was the bright shiny stone. They began pushing and shoving each other as they swam closer and closer.

Wait a minute said Trunks. Why are we fighting over the stone? Think about it. Who should have this stone more than anyone.

The elephants stopped and throught about what Trunks said. Suddenly they all shouted.

"Mom!" Lets give it to mom. She deserves it
more than any of us.

The three elephants took the stone , gathered
some vines and flowers, and made a beautiful
necklace for mom.

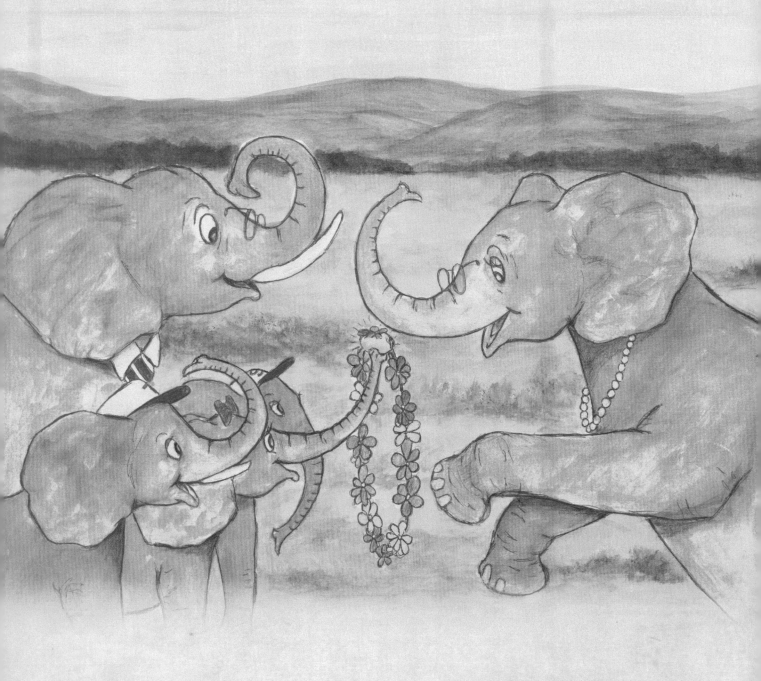

Mom was happy and thanked, Trunks, Snout
and Nosey. Father was also pleased.

He said , "children you are amazing. You really
did a fantastic job and learned a valuable
lesson. You learned to share and work together
as a team. I am super proud of you"

From that day forward Trunks, Snout and
Nosey remembered that children make parents
proud when they share ...and work together as
a team... to solve a problem.

Printed in the United States
by Baker & Taylor Publisher Services